The Wind in the Willows

an entertainment
based on the book by
Kenneth Grahame

Words by David Grant
Music by John Rutter

Kenneth Grahame's enchanting book *The Wind in the Willows* was first published in 1908 and has remained one of the best-loved of children's classics, enjoyed equally by generations of adult readers too. This musical adaptation was originally written as an 'entertainment' for The King's Singers (six male voices) and the City of London Sinfonia to perform at a family concert. The present published version, for five soloists, narrator and chorus, can either be performed as a concert piece or staged in various ways. Children can participate in the chorus (and as field-mice), though some altos, tenors and basses are essential. The main roles are intended for adult or teenage singers; Mole, a part originally written for male alto, could alternatively be sung by a boy alto, boy soprano, or baritone. The orchestral accompaniment is within the capacity of good teenage or amateur players; in the absence of orchestra, piano accompaniment would be adequate, with double-bass and drums if possible.

Music Department
OXFORD UNIVERSITY PRESS

for the King's Singers

THE WIND IN THE WILLOWS

Words by
DAVID GRANT

1: PROLOGUE

(Chorus)

Music by
JOHN RUTTER

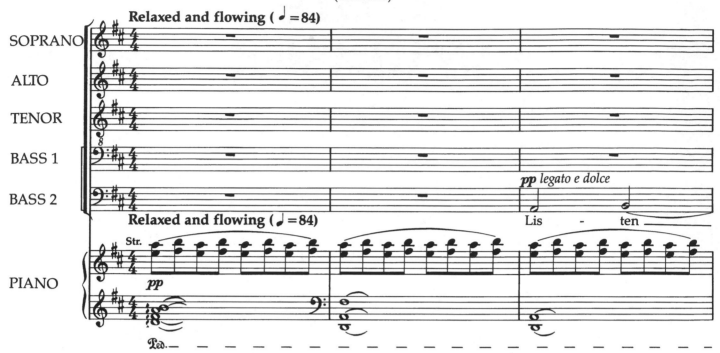

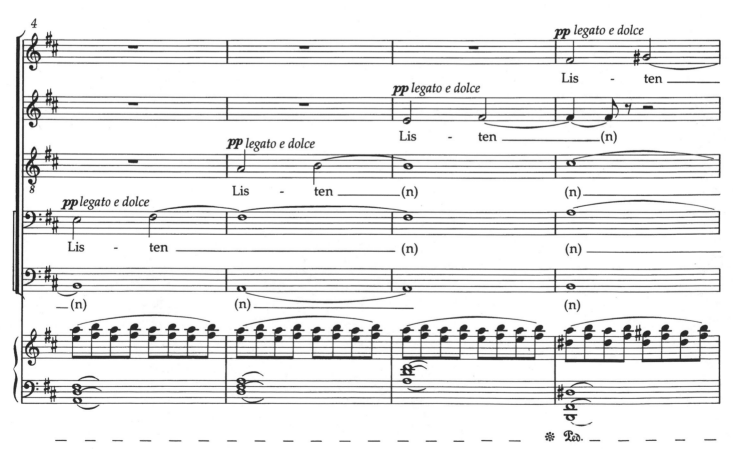

Printed in Great Britain

OXFORD UNIVERSITY PRESS, MUSIC DEPARTMENT, GREAT CLARENDON STREET, OXFORD, OX2 6DP

4

2: NARRATION

NARRATOR:

'Hang spring cleaning!' said Mole, flinging down his whitewash brush. 'Bother and blow!' said Mole, and he bolted out of the house, without even waiting to put on his coat. Something up above was calling him into the sunlight and away . . . across the meadows and alongside the copses . . . trotting along the river bank where, all of a sudden, he sat down, entranced and bewitched.

As he sat on the grass and looked across the river, he became aware of a bright little star winking at him from the opposite bank. The star became an eye . . . and then there was another eye . . . then a small brown face . . . with whiskers . . . (*Attacca No. 3*)

3: RIVER SCENE AND SONG

(Rat, Mole, and Chorus)

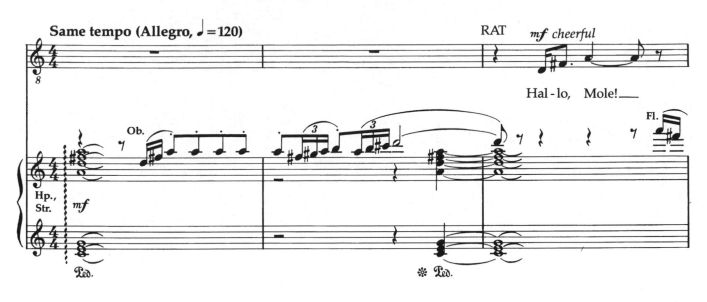

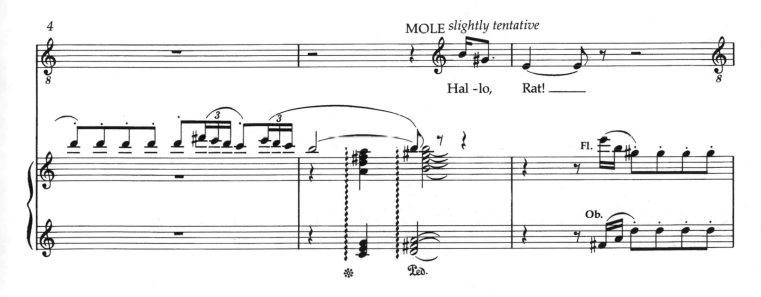

12

Hey ho! __ Rap - ture! __

fel - la who's a-float In his lit - tle wood - en boat?

C (RAT and MOLE with CHORUS)

Cu-cum-ber sand-wich-es, sa - vou - ry re - lish, Pa - té with truf - fles and cran-ber-ry jel - ly,

16

4: NARRATION

NARRATOR:

And so the two contented animals made their way slowly up the river to Rat's house. Rat spent the summer and the autumm showing Mole the sights of the River Bank, and introducing him to all his friends . . . except for one . . . the rather grumpy Mr Badger, who lived in the Wild Wood.

'Couldn't you invite him to dinner?' asked Mole.

'He wouldn't come,' said Rat. 'Simply hates Society.'

'Well then, why don't we go and call on him?' suggested Mole.

'It's a long journey,' replied Rat. 'But perhaps we *should* pay him a visit, especially as Christmas is coming on.'

So one cold December day they set off together through the Wild Wood, rather thoughtfully . . .

Alternative version of final sentence (to be used if No. 5 is omitted): So one cold December day they set off together through the Wild Wood, till they reached Badger's house.

*5: THE JOURNEY TO BADGER'S HOUSE
(The Wild Wood Carol)

(Rat and Chorus)

(Words by J. R.)

* This number may be omitted if it is desired to shorten the work.

4. And then an an-gel came down to earth To bear the news of the Sa-viour's birth; The first to mar-vel were shep-herds And sheep with their lambs. poor, (Hum)

23

6: AT BADGER'S HOUSE

(Mole, Rat, Badger, and Field-Mice)

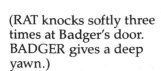

(RAT knocks softly three times at Badger's door. BADGER gives a deep yawn.)

(BADGER snores. RAT knocks again, louder. *Start music.*)

26

28

FIELD-MICE

then, a - las, they spoiled him.

Our

BADGER

I fear they must have spoiled him.

aun - tie says 'E tried to knock the vil - lage p'lice - man's

hel - met off, But then they foiled 'im!

RAT

It's a

BADGER

Be si - lent! It's a

con - duct is tru - ly ap - pal - ling. He's fool - ish and fi - ckle and ea - si - ly led, Con -

- cei - ted and boast - ful and weak in the head, He'll go to the bad and then soon he'll be dead:

What can we do _____ to pre - vent him from fall - ing? Last

month he bought a gip - sy ca - ra - van In bright ca - na - ry

34

* English sugar-coated confections

36

38

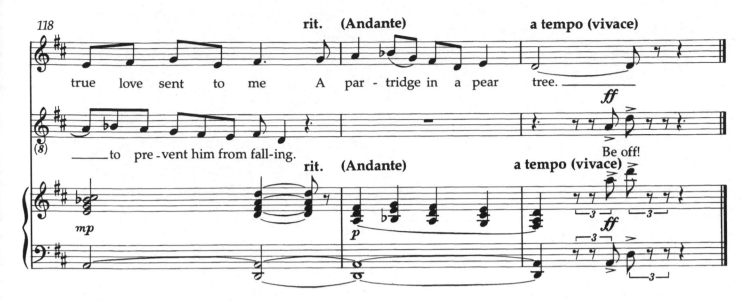

NARRATOR:

And that's how things were left. Rat and Mole returned home the next day, determined to save Toad from the dreadful consequences of his new motor car craze. The rest of the winter passed quietly, but one morning, quite early in the spring, all three animals happened to be standing in a peaceful lane near the river bank when they heard a most terrible commotion in the distance . . . (*End of narration to overlap with start of No. 7*)

7: TOAD'S CAR

(Chorus)

Note to conductor: What follows represents Toad's car (1908 vintage) already going fast as it becomes audible in the distance, getting nearer, slowing down and stopping. Allocate voices in whatever way works best.

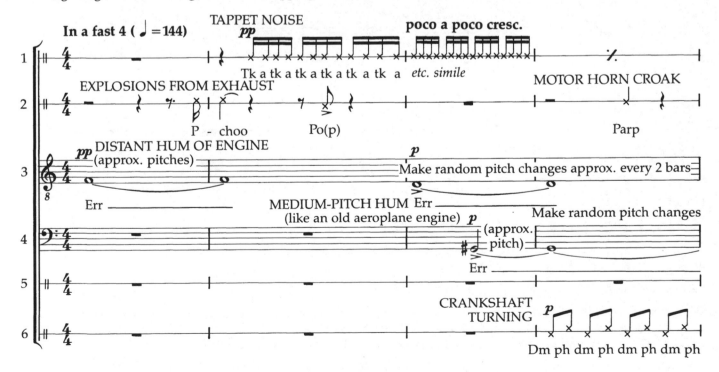

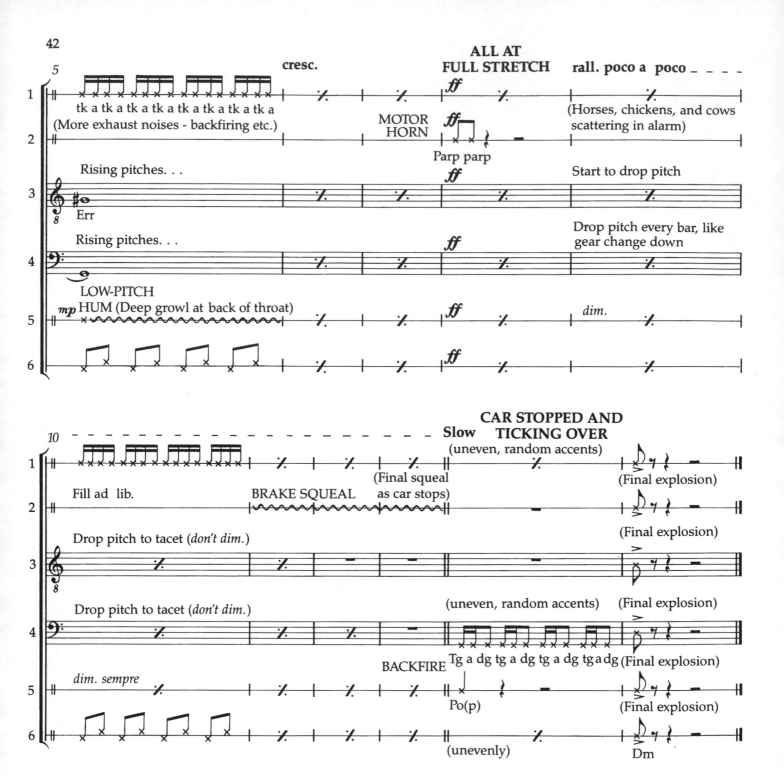

NARRATOR:

Sure enough, it was Toad; he jumped down from his car.

'I say, you chaps,' he said, 'what do you think of her? Straight eight, with sleeve valves of course . . . family crest on the door . . . does nearly fifty downhill!'

Badger interrupted sternly. 'Toad, you unhappy creature!'

'Me unhappy?' exclaimed Toad; 'What a lot of rot you do talk, Badger. Why, I'm the happiest creature alive! The open road . . . the smell of hot oil . . . if you chaps can't recognize the coming thing when you see it, then I'm afraid progress won't wait for you, and no more shall I . . . Must be off! See you all up at my place some time.'

And with that, Toad started up the car again and drove off. But that wasn't the end of it, as I'm afraid we shall see . . .

8: COURT SCENE
(Usher, Magistrate, Toad)

USHER: Silence! Silence in court!

* MAGISTRATE: Never in all my time as a
magistrate. . . never in all the long years I've

Marcia funebre (♩=60)

served on this bench. . . never has been seen a creature more abjectly despicable, a Toad
more steeped in the molasses of criminality, more tarred with the glue of felonious

turpitude than the hardened criminal we see melting like a fly-blown marshmallow before
our averted eyes. Pull yourself together, prisoner! Be a man, and prepare to hear your

sentence! You shall be taken from this place and be flung into the deepest, darkest, and
most vile-smelling dungeon that the resources of the County Gaol can provide. And there

* During the delivery of the Magistrate's speech, TOAD utters appropriate wails, groans, etc.

44

you shall languish, on the first count—stealing a motor car—ten years; on the second
count—driving in a most reckless and dangerous manner—fifteen years; on the

third count—insulting a policeman—twenty years. And in view of the seriousness
of the offences and the hardened criminality of the felon, I order that these terms

of imprisonment be served both consecutively and concurrently. . . Take him away!*

* Speech and music should finish at approximately the same time.

NARRATOR:

Toad, abject and downcast, was led away roughly by two horny-handed gaolers and thrown into the nastiest of dungeons, with nothing for company save the occasional spider, and no solace save that provided by a tin mug of brackish water and the stale crusts thrown to him from time to time . . . and, oh, I nearly forgot — the rather comely and kind-hearted daughter of one of the gaolers. Let us eavesdrop as she attempts to rally the starving and disconsolate felon . . .

9: IN PRISON

(Toad and Gaoler's Daughter)

46

48

37
Takes__ your ap - pe-tite ov - er the edge.__ Stewed mut - ton and

40
dump - lin's then,__ Just walk up and help your-self a-

42
- gain and a - gain:__ I bet you I got a few treats__ you nev - er

50

NARRATOR:

Nothing the gaoler's daughter had to offer seemed to rouse him. But like all great men of history, his single-mindedness saw him through. He escaped by exchanging clothes with a humble washerwoman; let us join him as he makes his way back to Toad Hall, a sadder and a wiser Toad . . . (*Narration continues over start of No. 10*)

10: ON THE ROAD TO TOAD HALL

(Toad and Chorus)

NARRATOR: . . . I'm not sure that's true, actually, but perhaps I'd better let you be the judge; here he is.

Bright, breezy and fast-moving (♩=144)

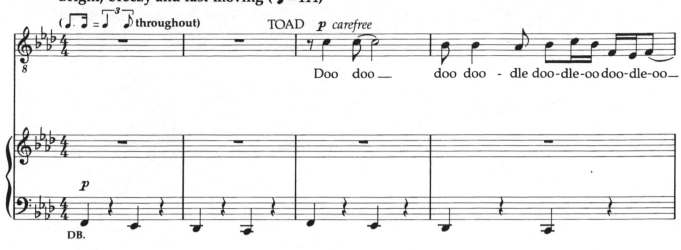

Doo doo — doo doo - dle doo-dle-oo doo-dle-oo

— doo doo doo doo-dle-oo doo — Doo doo — doo-dle-oo doo — doo-dle-oo

doo doo pa doo doo pa doo-dle-oo doo doo, — peep peep! I've got style, —

52

53

54

Oo ———————————— tell you how — Ssh! —

So stay a - while —— and —— I'll tell you how —— In the

strict - est con - fi - dence — I get called ———— by Scot - land Yard; — They

have to bring me in when a case gets too hard. Ein - stein took

56

58

wa   wa   doo   wa___   wa   wa

Doo   be doo   be doo   wa___   Doo   be doo

New-ton saw that ap - ple   drop from the tree,___   Well, he asked me what it meant, And I

Wow!   Oo _____

That's gra-vi-ty!___   said: Sci-ence and in - ven - tion ___ are most-ly due ___ To ___ Pro-

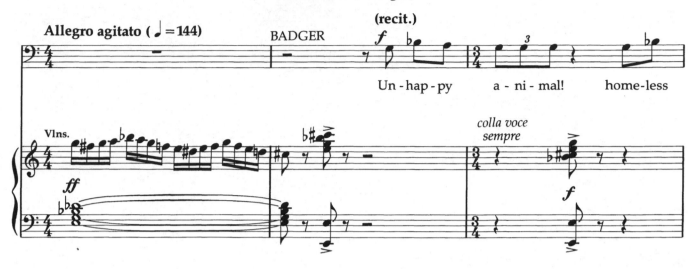

11: THE PLAN

(Mole, Toad, Rat, Badger)

64

66

MOLE

TOAD

RAT

BADGER *mf*

Now listen to me, Toad: all is not
lost, undeserving though you are...
colla voce

f freely

I have a plan.
colla voce

Allegro vivace (♩=144)

f

33

D

f

... with knives!

f

... with knives!

f

... with knives!

mf

We must arm our-selves with knives...   with

trem.

trem. sempre

p

sf

68

E accel.

cresc. sempre

-vance up-on the wea-sels and the fer-rets and the stoats, bran-dish-ing our wea-pons and

E accel.

p   cresc.

freely (recit.)   In tempo (♩=c. 112)

MOLE   p timidly

A fe-ro-cious and blood-cur-dling

TOAD   p timidly

A fe-ro-cious and blood-cur-dling

RAT   p timidly

A fe-ro-cious and blood-cur-dling

(BADGER)   freely (recit.)

sing-ing a fe-ro-cious and blood-cur-dling cho-rus.

freely (recit.)   In tempo (♩=c. 112)

f

f   p

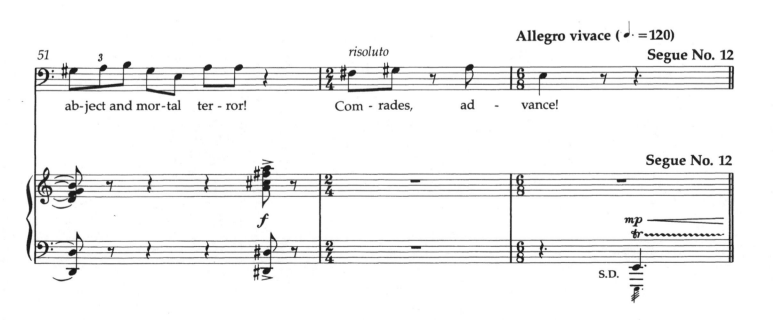

12: RECAPTURE OF TOAD HALL (Let's wallop a weasel)

(Mole, Toad, Rat, Badger)

72

* In this number, the shrieks and cries of the weasels, ferrets, and stoats are to be allocated to suitable members of the chorus.

13: NARRATION

NARRATOR:

Every last weasel, ferret and stoat fled in panic and disorder, and Toad Hall was once more Toad's. Badger lectured Toad sternly, reminding him that his folly and boastfulness had nearly cost him his liberty and his home, and Toad promised to mend his ways.

The next night a celebration banquet was held at Toad Hall, and everyone made merry. It was nearly midnight when Badger rose to his feet, rather unsteadily, and addressed the assembled company. (*Attacca No. 14*)

78

14: FINALE
(TOAD, BADGER, and CHORUS)

18

colla voce

ff

Hear, hear!

ff

BADGER

And now I call upon our good friend, Mr Toad, to make a brief re - ply.

colla voce

p

B (♩ = 104 sempre) *quiet and thoughtful*

21 **TOAD** *p legato sempre*

I could ne - ver have come back If it had-n't been for you, my friends;

sim.

p

25

A house can seem emp - ty, so you wan - der, And you think you've no friends . . .

There are so ma-ny things that I ne-ver real-ly saw be-fore,

But I think that I can see them clear-ly now:

The ket-tle on the hob, The chest-nuts in the fire, The

slip-pers by the rock-ing chair__ And wood-smoke drift-ing through the air. . . I

think that per-haps . . . It's time that per-haps . . . I star - ted, per-haps, To

think a - bout set - tl -ing down.

CHORUS

ALL VOICES

p dolce e legato

Home is a spe - cial kind of feel - ing:

The feel - ing of a place where you be - long;

84

know will al - ways cheer you, _____

gen - tle _____ fond 'hel - lo' _____ that seems to touch you with a

(A. T. B.) (Hum) _____ (Hum) _____

Like a

glow. _____ Home has a qui - et kind of

88

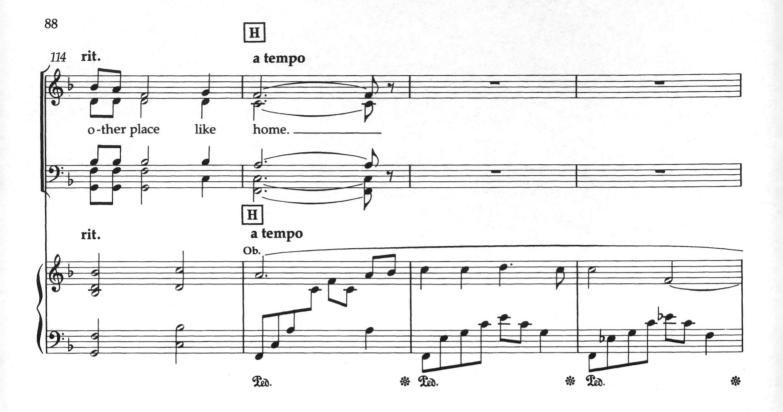

NARRATOR: Mole caught Rat's eye; Rat's eye caught Badger's eye. Each knew what home meant to the other. Nobody managed to catch Toad's

eye, but then Toad's eye was roving and resting lovingly an every detail of his home; worth a thousand gipsy caravans, worth a million motor cars, thought Toad.

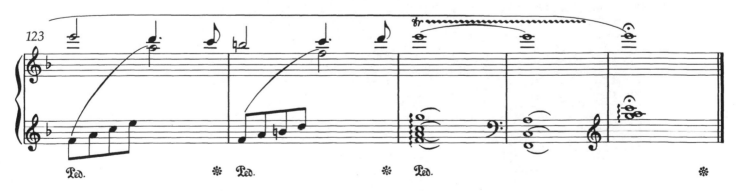